MEL BAY'S ROCK DRUMMING & SOLOING METHODS

by
Rob Leytham

CD CONTENTS

1	Quarter and Eighth Notes on the Drum Set [1:18]	18	Sixteenth-Note Ride Patterns [1:09]
2	Ride Cymbal, Bass Drum, and Hi Hat Exercises [1:04]	19	Drum Set Fills using Rolls [:49]
3	Quarter Note Hi Hat Exercises [1:08]	20	More Drum Set Fills using Rolls [:50]
4	Adding the Snare Drum [1:01]	21	Drum Set Patterns using Sixteenth Triplets [2:38]
5	Quarter Notes on the Hi Hat [1:01]	22	Sixteenth-Note Triplet Fill-ins [:59]
6	Quarter and Eighth Notes on the Snare Drum [:59]	23	More Sixteenth-Note Triplet Fill-ins [:58]
7	Basic Rock Beats [1:44]	24	Drum Set Beats using Paradiddles [:57]
8	Eighth-Note Drum Set Fill-ins [1:02]	25	Paradiddle Fill-ins [:57]
9	More Drum Set Fill-ins [1:04]	26	More Paradiddle Fill-ins [:56]
10	Drum Set Beats with Sixteenth Notes [1:00]	27	Spilled Coffee [1:16]
11	Sixteenth-Notes with the Bass Drum [1:08]	28	Bouncing Ball [1:31]
12	Sixteenth-Note Fill-ins [1:00]	29	Dancing Doctor Dennis [1:22]
13	More Sixteenth-Note Fill-ins [:58]	30	The Who Moon [1:23]
14	Advanced Sixteenth-Note Fill-ins [:57]	31	Bratcher Catcher [1:24]
15	Sixteenth-Note Beats with Snare and Bass [1:02]	32	Show Off [1:07]
16	Sixteenth-Note Beats on the Hi Hat [1:07]	33	Global Groove [1:50]
17	Ghost Notes [:58]	34	Funk-A-Diddle-Doo [1:20]

1 2 3 4 5 6 7 8 9 0

MEL BAY®

© 1997 BY MEL BAY PUBLICATIONS, INC., PACIFIC, MO 63069.
ALL RIGHTS RESERVED. INTERNATIONAL COPYRIGHT SECURED. B.M.I. MADE AND PRINTED IN U.S.A.

Visit us on the Web at http://www.melbay.com — E-mail us at email@melbay.com

*This book is dedicated to my beautiful
wife, Alyce, for all her support and love.*

*Also to my parents, Bob and Linda –
For all the years of encouragement and drum lessons.*

Also special thanks should go to the following: my sister Tonya (all those years of having to listen to me practice), Herb and Audra Leytham, Ray and Mae McCollum, Tom May, Bennie Stofer, Tim O'Neal and John Becker at Premier Perc., Dana Cox at Sabian, Jack Wells, Allen, Doug, Bob, Bill, Steve and Clay at Antioch Music Center, Bill Cardwell at C&C DrumShop, Bruce Bergh, Dennis Norton, Andrew Moore, Dr. Phil Posey, Dr. Dennis Rogers, Paul Smith, Matt and Carol Curtis, Mr. William Bay, and William F. Miller and Ronald Spagnardi at Modern Drummer. I also thank God for giving me the opportunity to teach so many wonderful students. I am truly blessed!

Introduction

In rock music today, the drummer is required to be more than just the time keeper. Gone are the days when all a drummer had to do was play eighth notes on the hi hat and hit the snare on beats "two" and "four." Today, rock drummers need to be more technical and musical in their approach to their instrument.

It is just as important to be able to play 16th notes with the bass drum as it is on the snare. The drummer's rhythmic vocabulary must include everything from quarter notes to 16th-note triplets to 32nd notes and, most importantly, be able to play them in time. Drum set fill-ins and solos must be as melodic and musical as they are exciting. This book will help teach these ideas and techniques by starting with quarter-note and eighth-note exercises on the drum set. Following exercises will include 16th notes, 16th-note triplets, 32nd notes, Paradiddles, and finally ending with some fun and challenging drum set solos.

When practicing with this book, always make sure that you have a firm grasp of the technique being studied before moving on. Don't rush yourself, it takes time and practice. Try to practice 30 minutes a day, and if you can, get with a good teacher. Most importantly, have fun with your instrument! There is not an exercise or a solo in this book that is worth getting frustrated over. Always enjoy creating music.

Notation Key

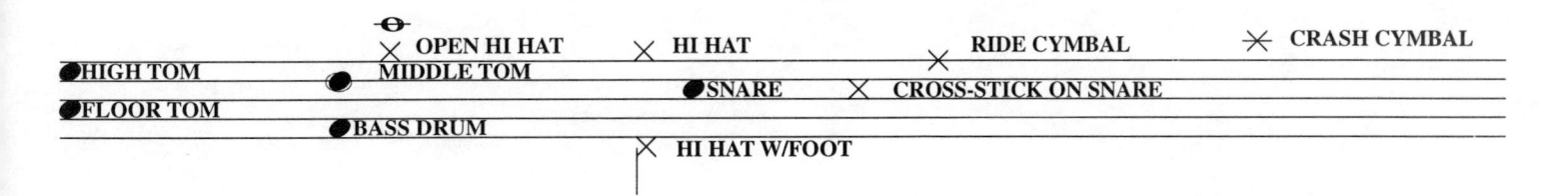

- HIGH TOM
- MIDDLE TOM
- FLOOR TOM
- BASS DRUM
- OPEN HI HAT
- HI HAT
- RIDE CYMBAL
- CRASH CYMBAL
- SNARE
- CROSS-STICK ON SNARE
- HI HAT W/FOOT

Table of Contents

1. Quarter & 8th Note Study on Drum Set 5

2. Drum Set Beats & Fills using 16th Notes 11

3. Drum Set Fills using Rolls 20

4. Drum Set Beats & Fills using 16th Triplets 22

5. Drum Set Beats & Fills using Paradiddles 26

6. Drum Set Solos 29

Quarter and Eighth Notes on the Drum Set

Ride Cymbal and Bass Drum Exercises

We will start applying quarter and eighth note rhythms to the drum set. The next few pages will help develop your coordination technique. Place your right stick on the ride cymbal and play an even eighth-note rhythm. Strike the cymbal about five inches from the edge. This will ensure that you will not get too many overtones, sometimes called a "cymbal wash." Add your bass drum to the exercises by first repeating each measure four to eight times before repeating each line twice. When striking the bass drum, make sure that the beater comes off the drum head as soon as the note is played. This will help in the development of a faster and more controlled foot.

Ride Cymbal, Bass Drum and Hi Hat Exercises

One of the hardest techniques to develop on the drum kit is the addition of playing the hi hat with the foot. We will start out slow by only playing it on beats "two" and "four." When playing the hi hat with the foot, you need to develop a "rocking" motion. Have your heel down on beats "one" and "three." On beats "two" and "four" the toe will go down and the heel up, producing a good "chick" sound from the hi hat. Play the next exercises repeating each measure four to eight times before repeating each line twice. Make sure that you listen to the sound that your hi hat is producing.

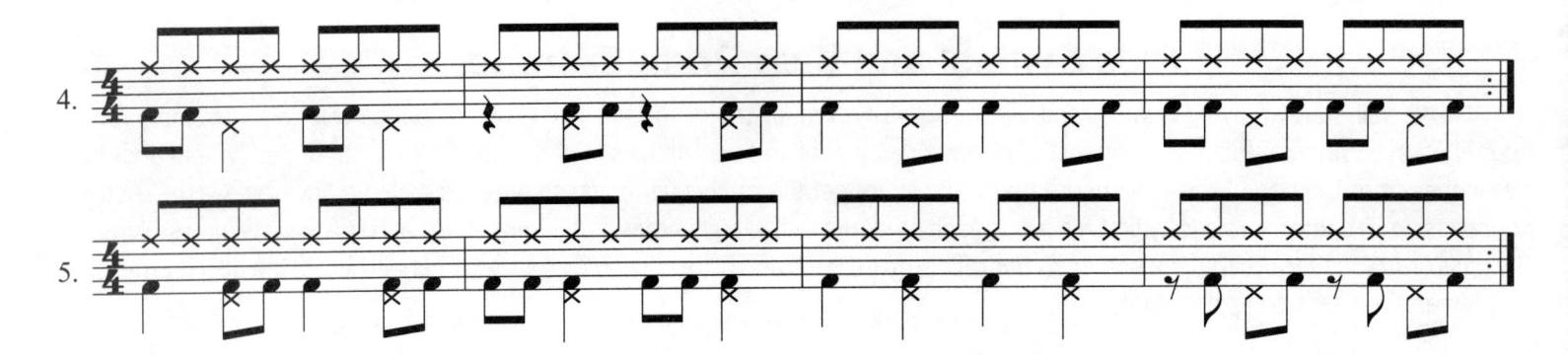

Quarter Note Hi Hat Exercises

Play these next exercises with the hi hat playing quarter notes with the foot. You can continue the "rocking" motion with the foot. The toe will come down and the heel up to produce the "chick" sound for the quarter notes. The heel will go down and the toe up on the "&'s." You can also keep the heel up with the toe down, lifting and dropping the leg slightly on the quarter notes. It is best to use that technique when playing at faster tempos. Practice each exercise at an even tempo, repeating each measure four to eight times before repeating each line twice.

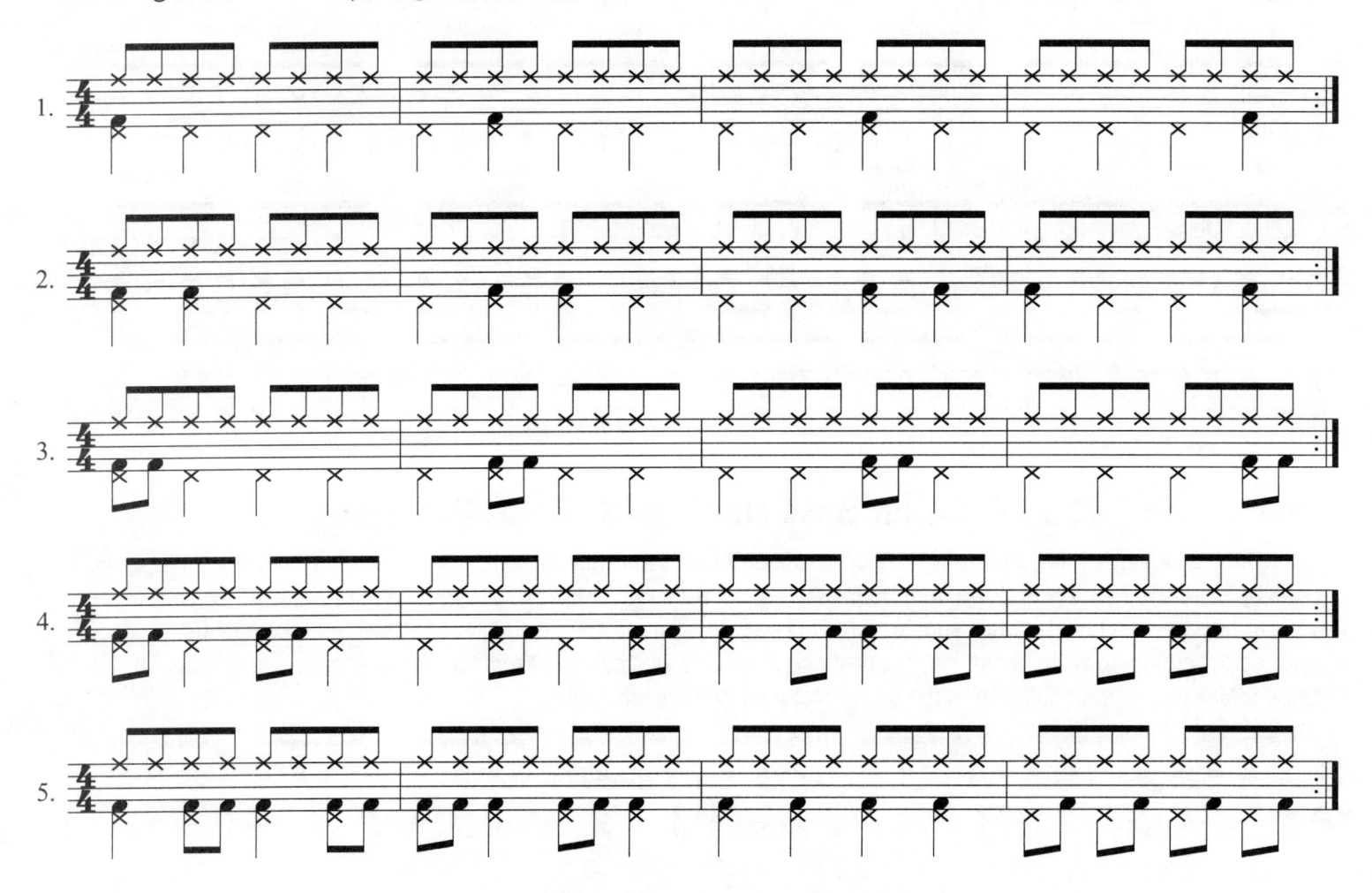

Adding the Snare Drum

On the next set of exercises, we will have all four limbs playing rhythms on the drum set. The ride cymbal will continue playing straight eighth notes. The bass drum will play a variety of quarter and eighth notes. The hi hat and the snare drum will play on beats "two" and "four." Make sure that you rock your foot when playing the hi hat. After striking the snare drum, remember to lift the stick from the head immediately. This will ensure that you won't get any unnecessary snare bounces or arm pain due to the repeated shock of the stick being forced through the drum head. Again, repeat each measure four to eight times before repeating each line twice.

Quarter Notes on the Hi Hat

Play these next drum set coordination exercises with the hi hat playing quarter notes with the foot. Repeat the continuous patterns played by the ride cymbal, snare drum, and hi hat several times before adding the bass drum.

Quarter and Eighth Notes on the Snare Drum

The next exercises will have the snare drum playing a variety of quarter and eighth note rhythms while the ride cymbal, bass drum, and hi hat play a repeated pattern. Get comfortable with the ride cymbal, bass, and hi hat patterns by practicing them alone before adding the snare rhythms.

Basic Rock Beats to be Memorized

Take the next 10 exercises and try to memorize them. These are beats that you will play in bands for the rest of your drumming career. Of course there are many more beats to learn, but these are your basic rock beats. The first six exercises will be played with the right hand on the ride cymbal. The last four exercises will have the right hand playing straight eighth notes on the closed hi hat. Notice that on the last four exercises, we are incorporating snare "cross sticking." Turn the drum stick around and lay the tip of the stick on the snare. Hold on to the stick with your hand cupped. Strike the rim of the snare drum with the butt of the stick without lifting the tip. This will produce a wood-like sound. This technique is used in Latin, country, and soft ballad music. Play these beats to your favorite groups and recordings. Also find some friends who play guitar and bass and start forming your band.

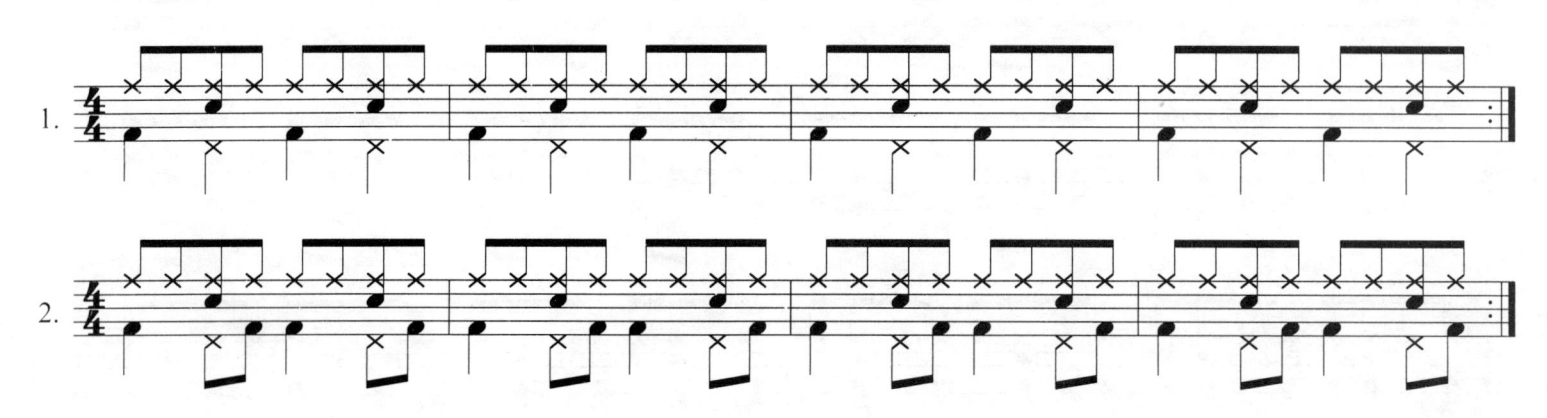

Eighth-Note Drum Set Fill-ins

Fill-ins are the exciting things drummers do to connect musical phrases. They connect verses to choruses and visa-versa. Fill-ins usually happen at the end of a four or eight-measure musical phrase. Chances are that you became interested in drumming because of hearing a cool fill-in that the drummer did during one of your favorite songs. Practice these exercises by playing three measures of a basic rock beat and going straight into the fill without hesitating. Try to keep your feet playing quarter notes on the bass drum and hi hat to ensure that you don't speed up during the fill. Drummers speeding up during a fill-in is a common complaint that many guitarists and band leaders have. Try to use several different memorized beats while playing this page.

More Drum Set Fill-ins

The next group of fill-ins will incorporate eighth notes, eighth rest, quarter notes, and quarter rest. Again practice with three measures of a rock beat, then one measure of fill-in. Make sure that your feet continue playing the quarter notes on the bass and hi hat.

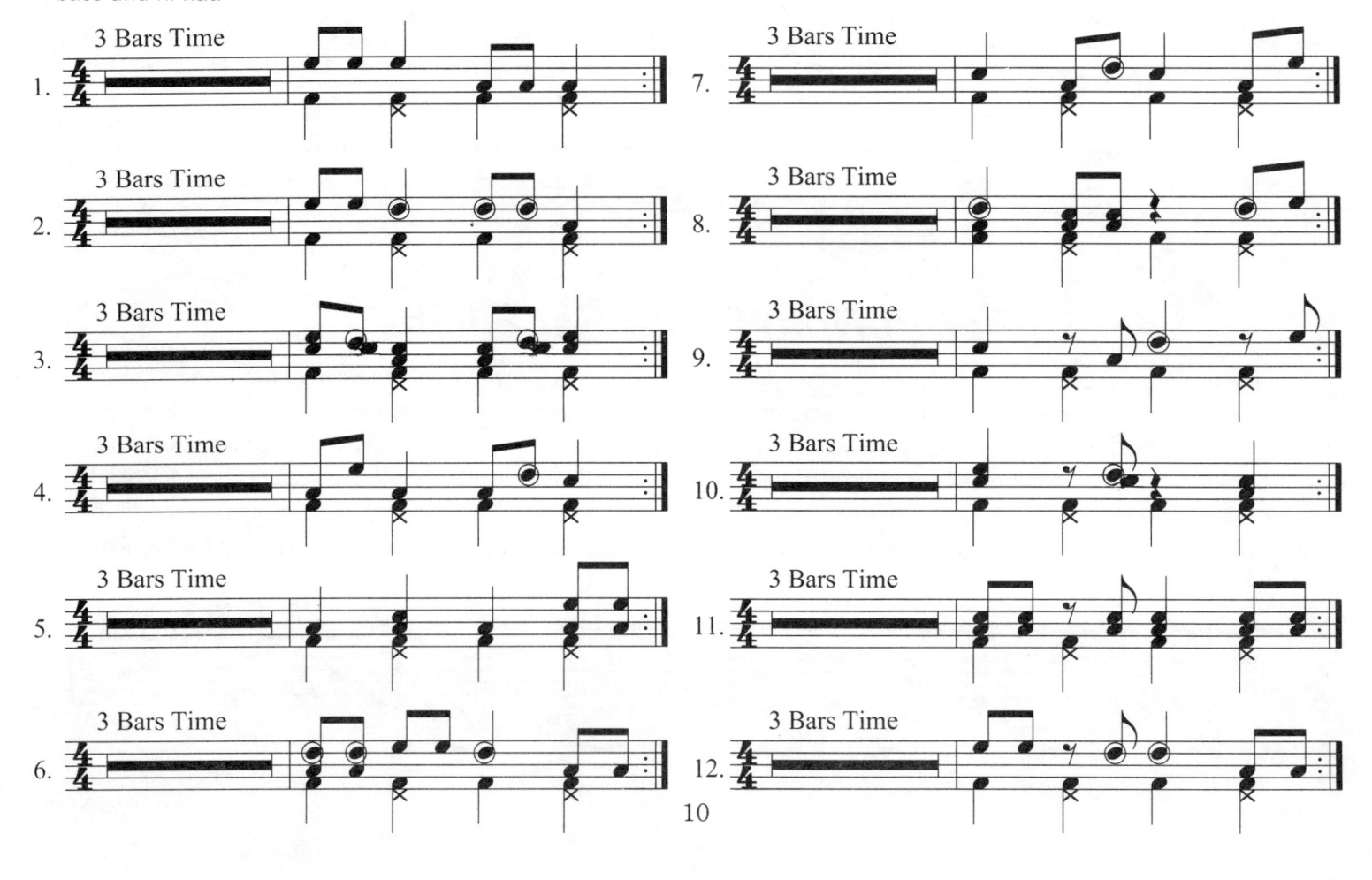

Drum Set Beats with Sixteenth Notes

Practice the next five exercises with straight eighth notes played on the ride cymbal. Notice that the snare will be struck on beats "two" and "four" along with sixteenth notes placed between the ride-cymbal rhythm. Make sure that you don't accidentally strike the ride cymbal when playing the 16th on the snare. When you are comfortable playing the rhythms with your hands, add the bass drum and hi hat. Play these beats at different tempos and make sure you memorize them.

The next five exercises are more melodic. The left hand will strike the high tom on the notated "ah's" of a beat. The floor tom will be struck on the notated "e's" and the snare drum struck on beats "two" and "four."

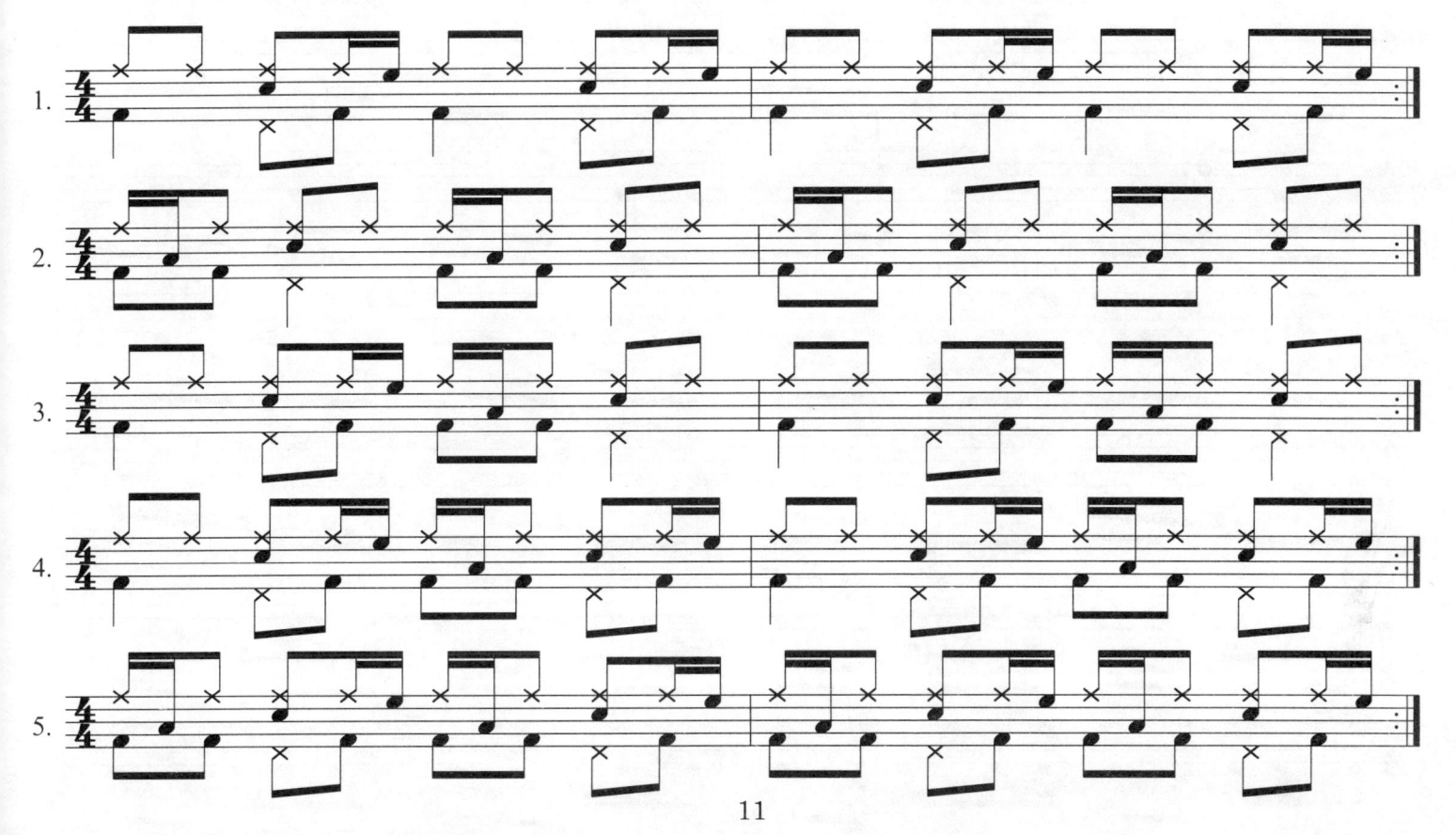

Sixteenth Notes with the Bass Drum

Practice the next 12 exercises with straight eighth notes played on the ride cymbal. The bass drum will play a variation of eighth and 16th notes. Practice the ride cymbal and bass drum first before adding the snare and hi hat. After you are comfortable playing the bass drum rhythms, add the snare and hi hat on beats "two" and "four." Practice these exercises at different tempos and memorize your favorite beats.

Sixteenth-Note Fill-ins

Play three bars of time using the beats that you already have memorized. After playing the three bars of time, add the 16th-note fill-in. Make sure that you don't hesitate going from the beat into the fill-in. Try to play a variety of different beats.

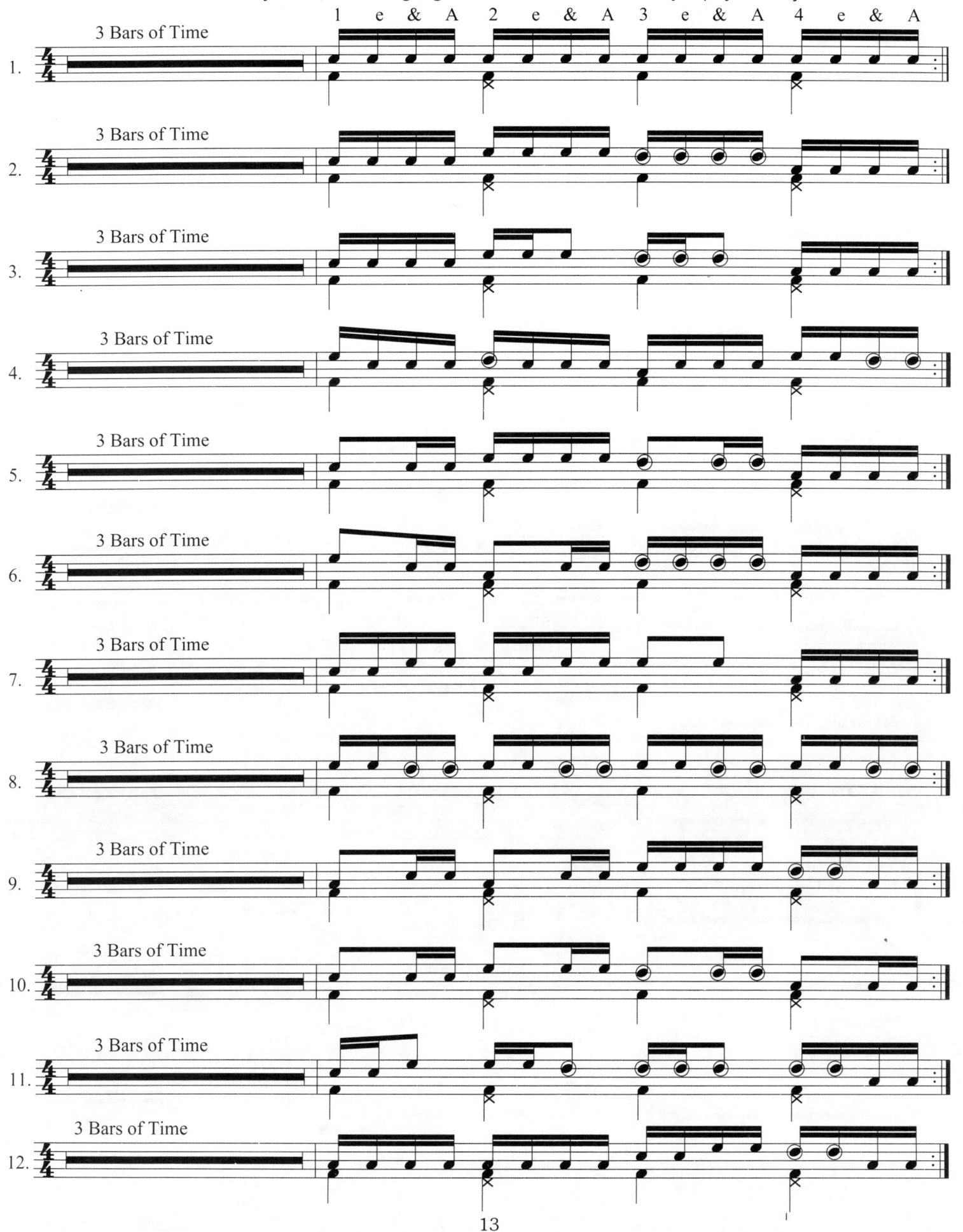

More Sixteenth-Note Fill-ins

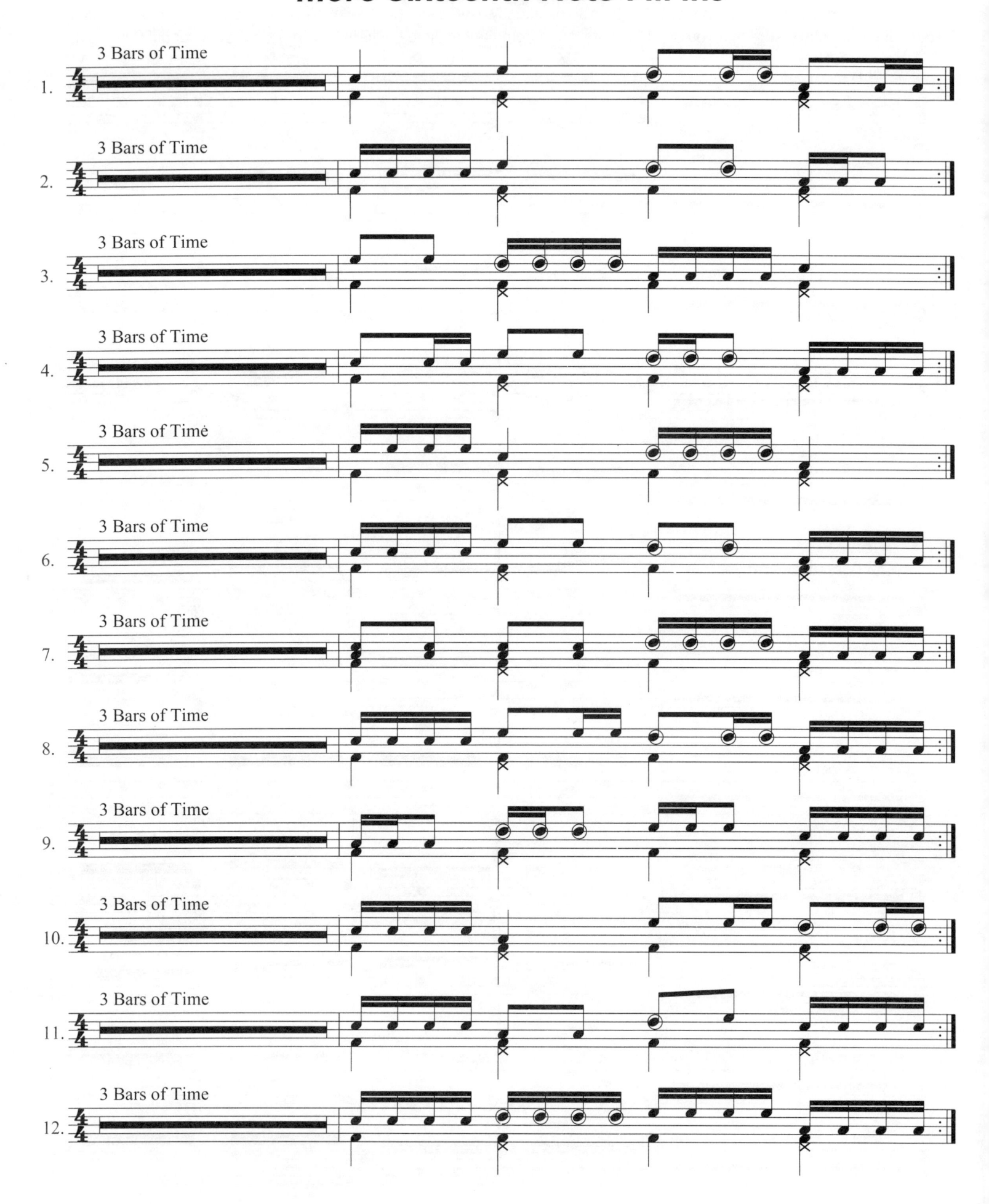

Advanced Sixteenth-Note Fill-ins

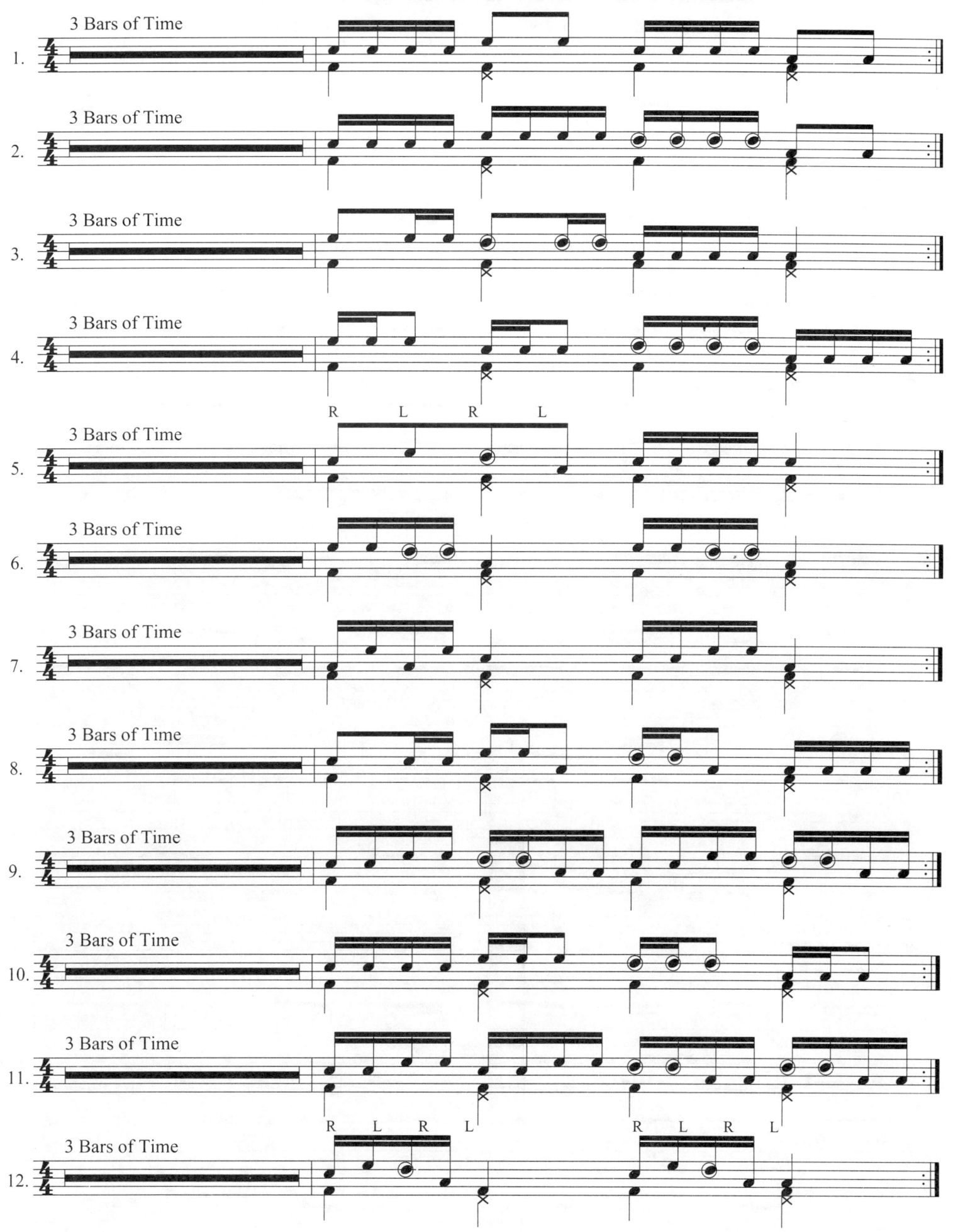

Sixteenth-Note Beats with Snare and Bass

The next 10 exercises are combinations of 16th notes played between the snare drum and bass drum on the first measure. The second measure is more melodic with the addition of the high tom and floor tom. Learn these exercises slowly before building up speed.

Sixteenth-Note Beats on the Hi Hat

Play the next 12 exercises with the hands playing alternating 16th notes on the hi hat. On the first eight exercises the snare drum will be struck on beats "two" and "four." The bass drum will play a variety of quarter, eighth, and 16th-note rhythms. The last four exercises will have the snare and toms playing 16th notes amongst the hi hat 16ths. Make sure that the hands continue to alternate when practicing these exercises.

Ghost Notes

Practice the alternating 16th notes with the right hand on the hi hat and left hand on the snare drum. Notice that there are "( )" around the left-hand snare hits. This means that the left hand will lightly strike the snare. This is sometimes called a "ghost stroke" and is used a lot in funk, fusion, and some rock. The right hand will play the eighth notes on the hi hat, but will also strike the snare on beats "two" and "four." These notes are to be accented. Now add the bass drum rhythms to each exercise.

Sixteenth-Note Ride Pattern

Sometimes a drummer does not want to play just straight eighth notes on the ride cymbal or closed hi hat. Eighth notes might make the music feel "jagged," and the music might call for a different feel. Adding a 16th note between the two eighth notes will allow the drummer's groove to flow nicer. First learn the 16th-note ride cymbal pattern before adding the other limbs. Count the ride cymbal pattern "1-e-&, 2-e-&, 3-e-&, 4-e-&." After you are comfortable playing that rhythm, add the snare, bass, and hi hat to these exercises. These beats can be used in a lot of Latin, funk, rock, and fusion music.

Drum Set Fills using Rolls

Let us take the rudiments and apply them to the drum set. When playing the three bars of time, try to include some double strokes on the hi hat. Two examples have been given, but try to come up with your own. Make sure that the double strokes on the toms are clean and even. The "Drop-Pull" technique is very important in playing double strokes on a tom tom.

More Drum Set Fills using Rolls

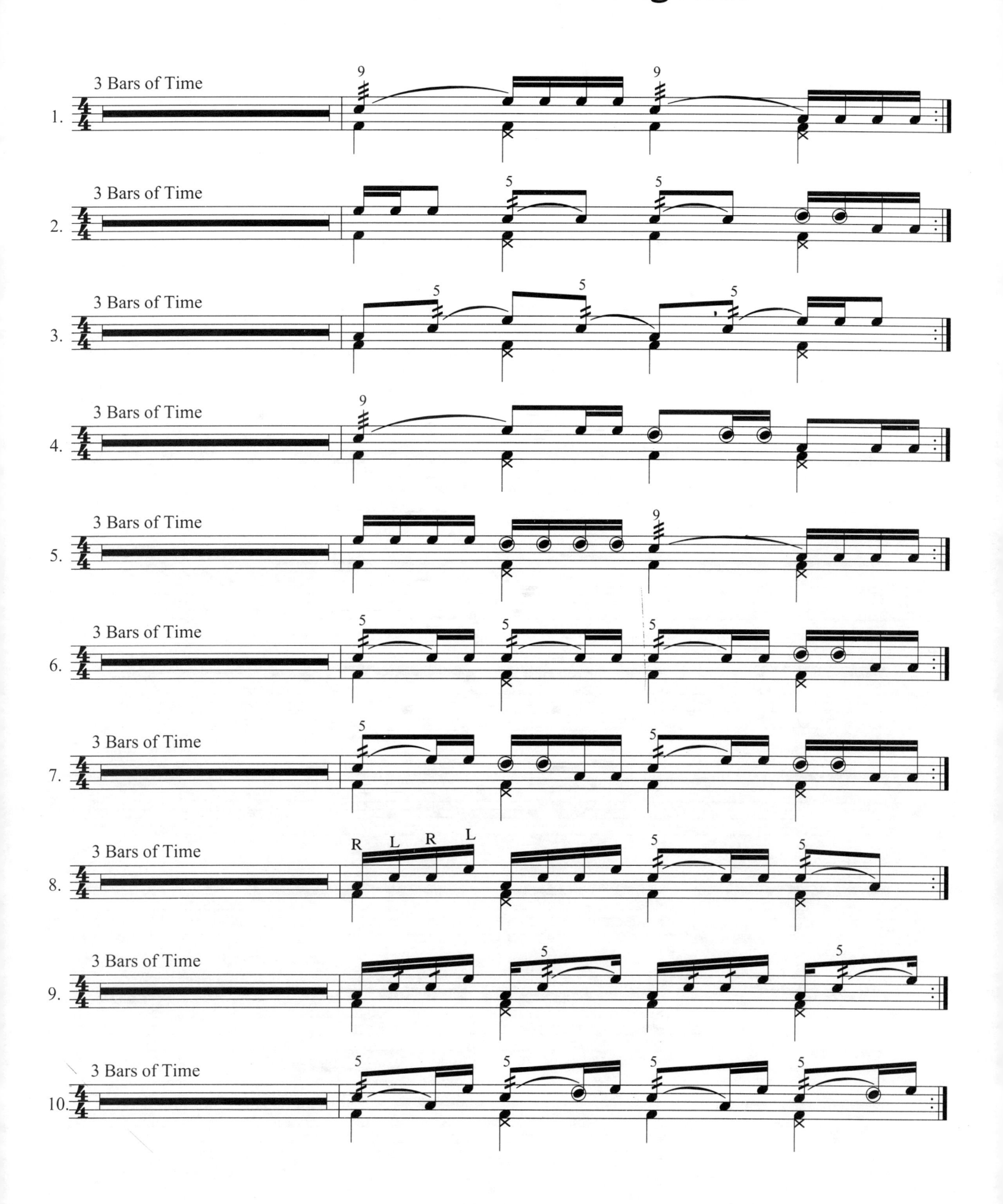

Drum Set Patterns using 16th-note Triplets

Practice the next set of beat exercises using 16th-note triplets. These triplets will be played by using a controlled double with either the hand or the foot. If it is done with the hand, make sure that the triplets remain even in sound. Don't play the double stroke too fast. If the triplet is played by using a double on the bass drum, make sure that the tempo does not vary.

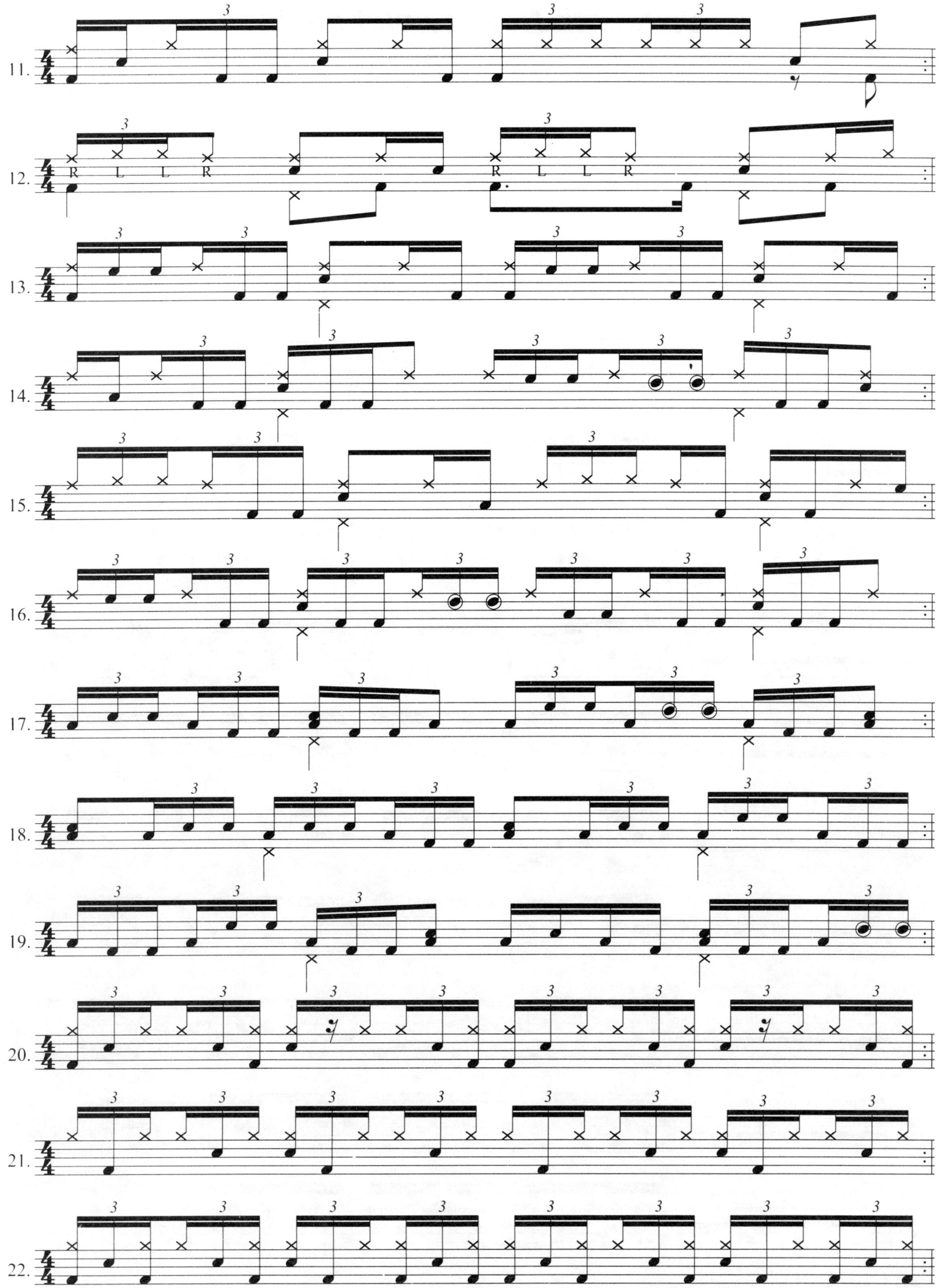
11.
12.
R L L R R L L R
13.
14.
15.
16.
17.
18.
19.
20.
21.
22.

Sixteenth-Note Triplet Fill-ins

Play the next set of fill-ins using 16th-note triplets. Play three measures of a beat and then play the fill-in. Make sure that you play both the beat and the fill at the same tempo. Sometimes when using 16th-note triplets in a fill, the tempo can lose speed. Be aware of your time.

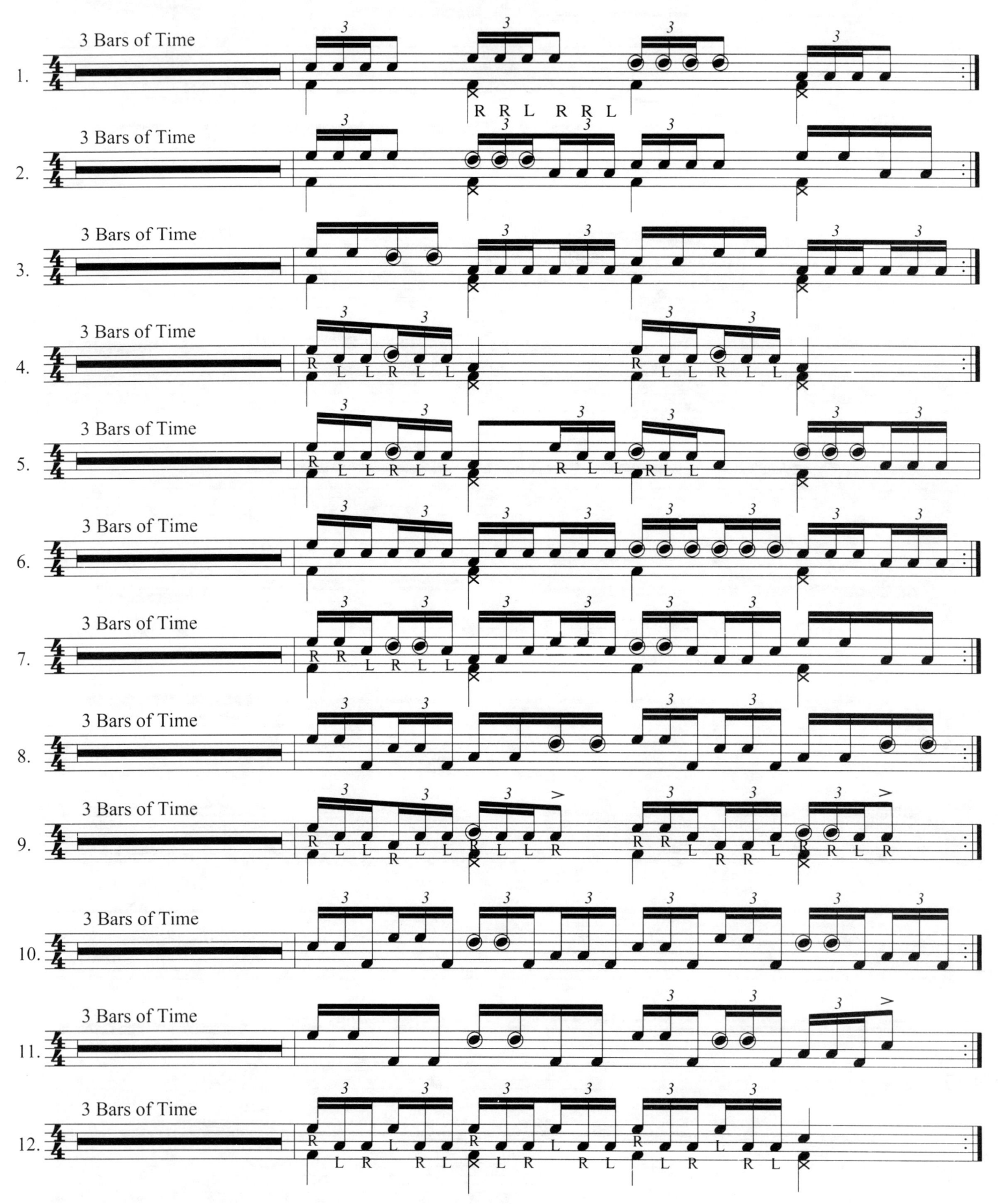

More Sixteenth-Note Triplet Fill-ins

Drum Set Beats using Paradiddles

Learn the next set of drum beats using single paradiddles around the drum set. Make sure that the single and double strokes are played as even 16ths. Learn the hand patterns before adding your feet.

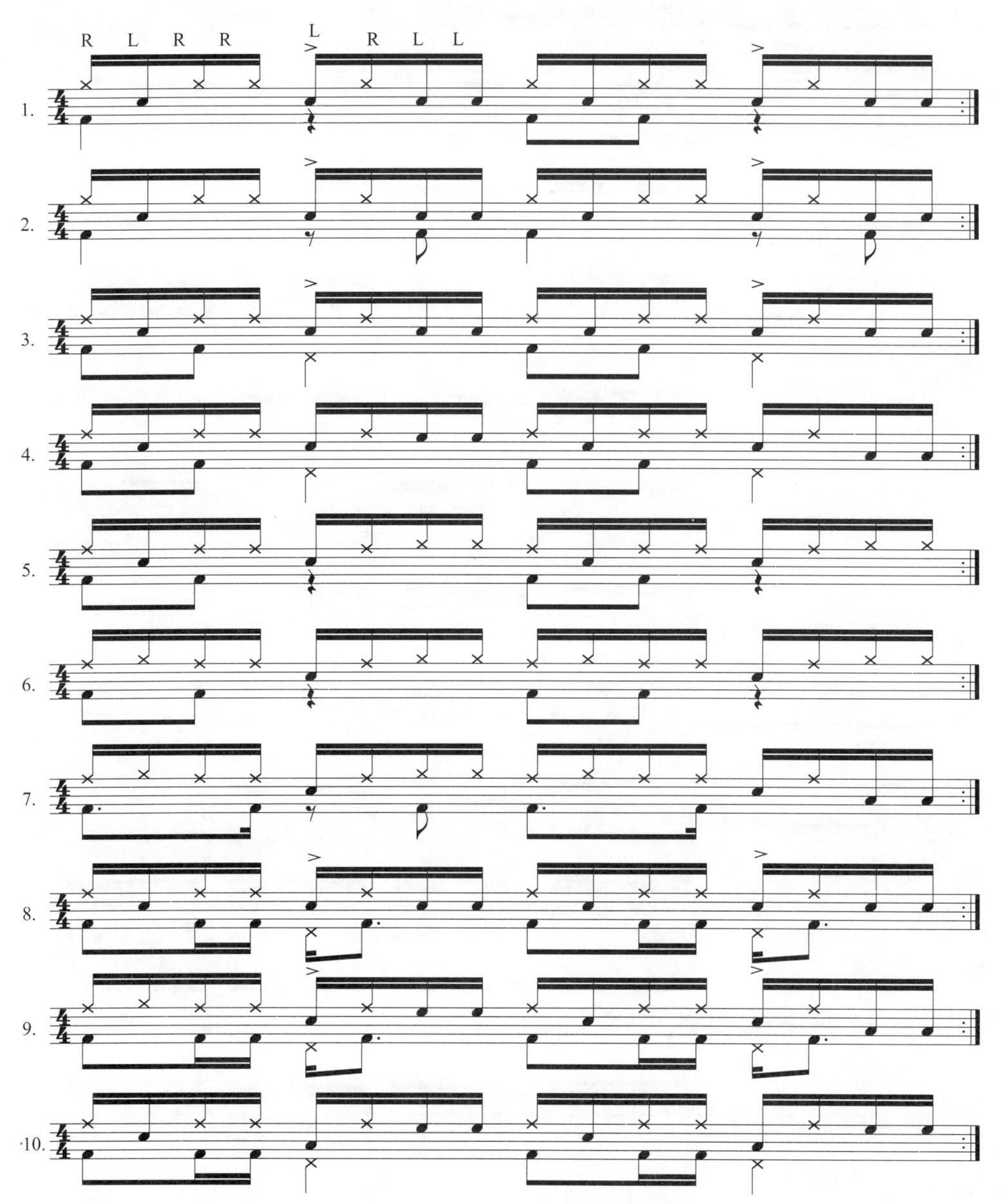

Paradiddle Fill-ins

The next set of drum fill-ins will incorporate paradiddles. Some of the paradiddles will be played using straight 16th notes while others will be 16th-note triplets. Make sure that the fills are played at the same tempo that the three measures of time are. Try to use a variety of different beats.

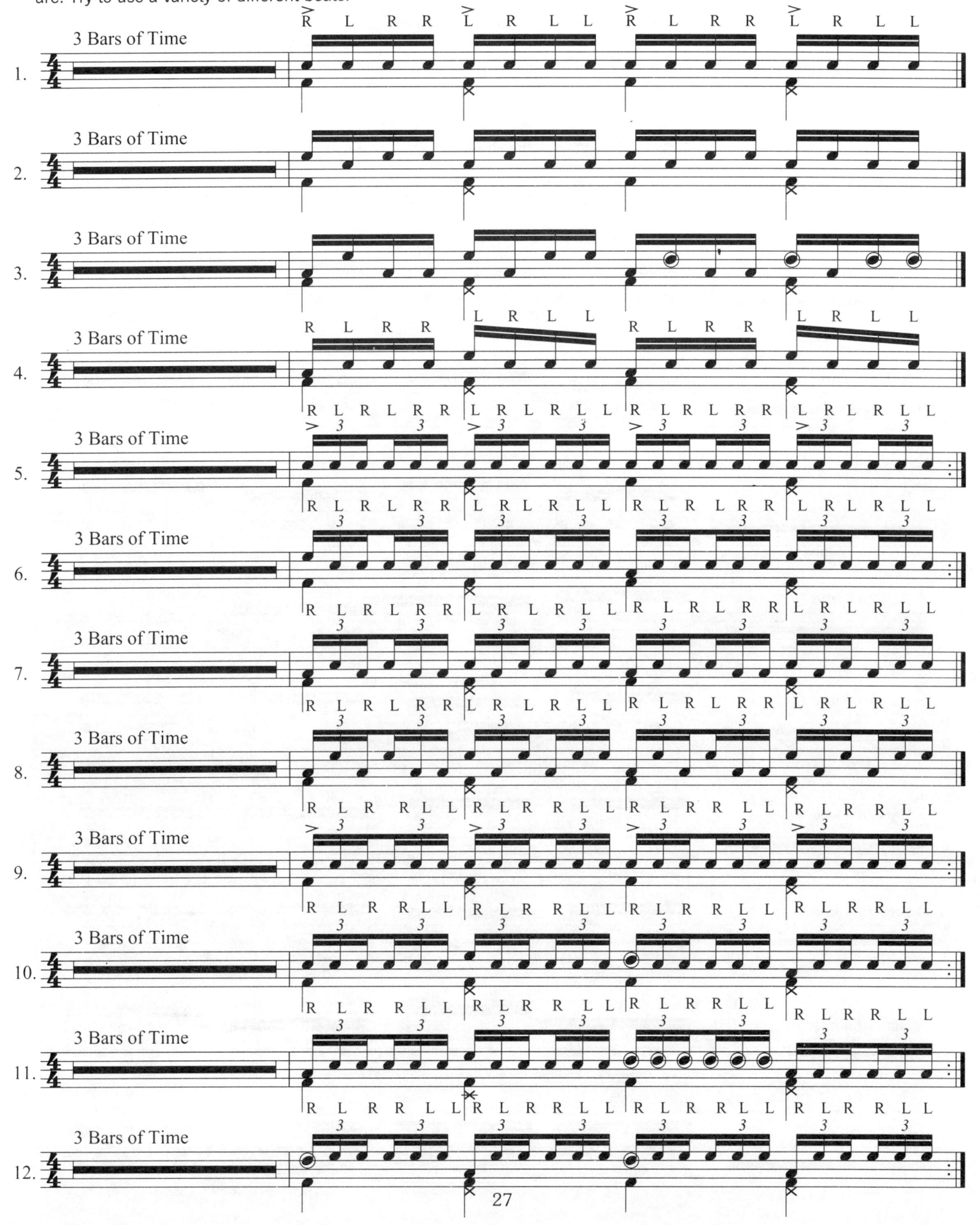

More Paradiddle Fill-ins

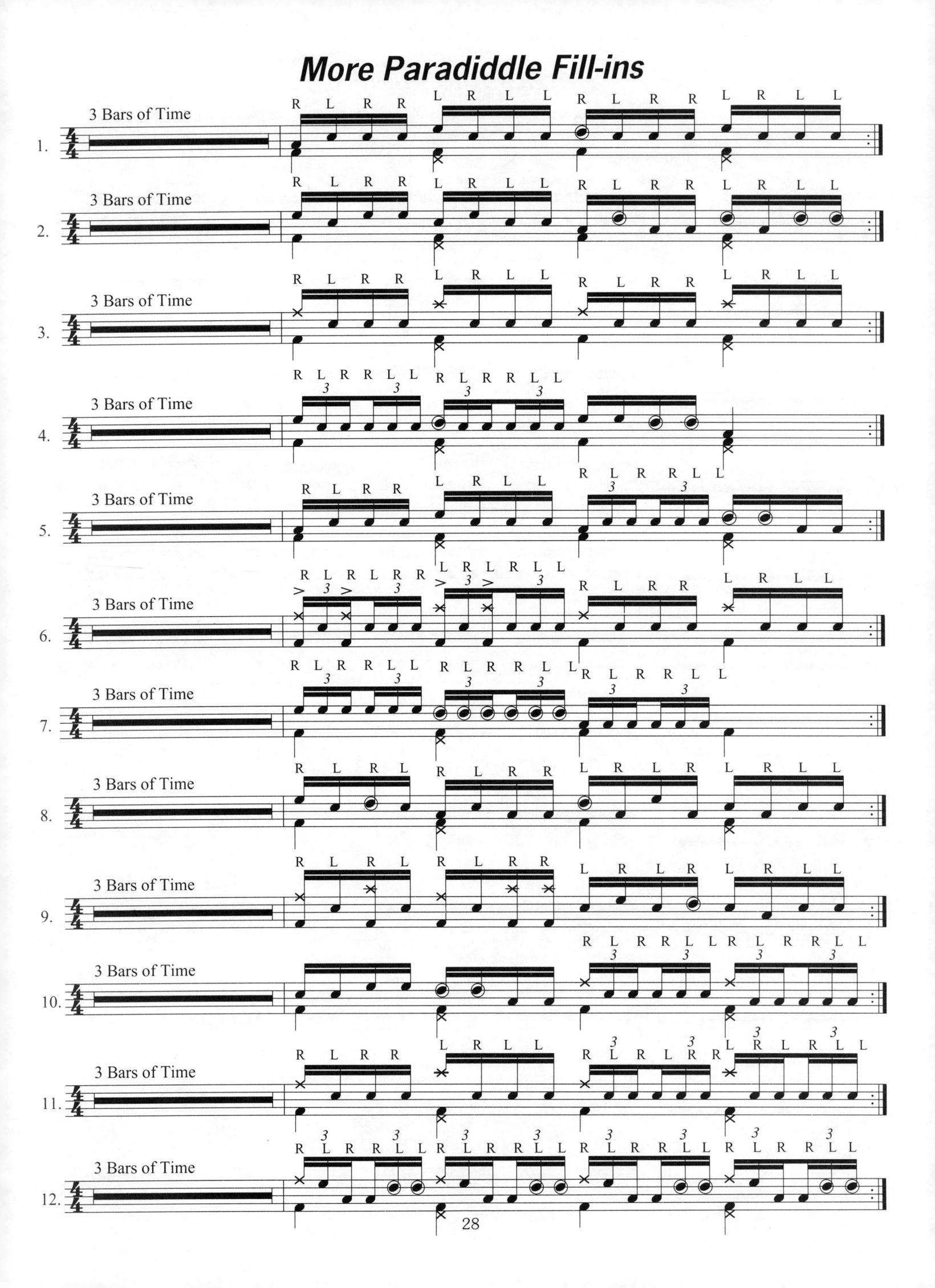

SPILLED COFFEE

BOUNCING BALL

DANCING DOCTOR DENNIS

THE WHO MOON

BRATCHER CATCHER

SHOW OFF

FUNK-A-DIDDLE DOO

GLOBAL GROOVE

37